A Special Gift

For:

From:

Date:

OLD AVILES STREET (SPANISH QUARTER) ST. AUGUSTINE, FLORIDA 22

THE OLDEST CITY IN THE UNITED STATES

OLD ST. AUGUSTINE
THROUGH THE CENTURIES

Randy Cribbs

River Press, LLC
St. Augustine, Florida
www.randycribbsauthor.com

OLD ST. AUGUSTINE
THROUGH THE CENTURIES

Copyright 2015 by Randy Cribbs

All rights reserved. No part of this book may be reproduced, stored in a retrieval system or transmitted in any form, electronic, mechanical, or by other means, without written permission of the author.

Library of Congress Control Number: 2015943459

ISBN: 978-0-9849909-0-0

Several poems in this publication first appeared in
'Ancient City Treasures' by Randy Cribbs,
copyright 2006

Published by River Press, LLC
Printed in the United States of America

To obtain books go to www.randycribbsauthor.com; www.amazon.com; www.bn.com or write River Press, LLC.

52 Tuscan Way

Ste 202, # 404

St. Augustine, Florida 32092

Contents

Welcome 10

Ancient City 12

Aviles Street 14

Imagine 16

Tolomato 18

Oldest Drugstore 20

Old Jail 22

Old Town Streets 24

Castillo de San Marcos 26

Lighthouse Porch 28

Oldest House 30

Lasting 32

Plaza Beginning 34

Renovation 36

Oldest Schoolhouse 38

Fountain of youth 40

Bridge of Lions 42

Nombre de Dios 44

St Johns River 46

Barracks 48

Bartram Trail Incident 50

Lovers' Wall 52

Spanish Military Hospital 54

Menendez	56
Drake's Raid	58
Flagler	60
Chieftain	62
Timucua	64
Ghosts	66
Carriage	68
Alligator Farm	70
Early on St. George Street	72
St. George Street	74
The Other End	76
Finally	78

Author's Note

In 1565, Pedro Menendez de Aviles, Spain's most experienced admiral, founded St. Augustine. When the Pilgrims subsequently came ashore at Plymouth, St. Augustine was already a town with a fort, church, seminary, hospital, fish market, and about 120 shops and houses. It is indeed the nation's oldest city.

Through modern verse and antique postcards, this book offers an inner perspective of significant characters, places, and events that give St. Augustine its' unique personality.

Randy Cribbs

Many thanks to these good friends for their valuable contributions:

Ed Wilks   www.legaciesandmemoriespublishing.com

John Bouvier   www.griffons.com

Henry Hird II   www.augustine.com

Kenneth M. Barrett, Jr. www.floridaheritagephotography.com

Books by Randy Cribbs

'Where You There? Vietnam Notes'

'Tales from the Oldest City'

'One Summer in the Old Town'

'Illumination Rounds'

'The Vessel ... Tinaja: An Ancient City Mystery'

'Ancient City Treasures'

'Ghosts: Another Summer in the Old Town'

'Just A Dog and the Musings of His Pet'

'Old St. Augustine ... Through the Centuries'

'Everything Is'

for dad

Welcome

To capture the essence
of the Old Town, you
must look into her soul
for the stories
yet to be told,
waiting down the
narrow, worn streets
where the past
and you can meet
at places often passed
but not seen,
where you will
feel what it means
to enter the heart,
that beats to the echo
of hooves pulling a cart,
among whispers of the past
and things meant to last,
urging your imagination
be set free;
only then
will you truly see.

Ancient City

The Old Town is
not old at all
by some standards –
young, in the worldly
scheme of things.

But here, in this land,
it is the oldest.
Already a half-century old,
boasting a town with a
fort, shops, houses, when
those fleeing persecution
landed on that rock,
   further north..

Unique in that it is old
now, today, measured
by history, preserved in
places and rooms soaked
by smells and voices of times past,
   and more.

Downtown, Old Town, city proper,
where buildings are not so old,
but neither are they young,
even there, the aura of history,
the past, other times,
prevail.
You feel it. Sense it.

It enters you
with a mystique
in the air that
seems to rush down
the narrow streets.

"You have such a unique town,"
I have been told.
The intent to convey
something special,
something words alone
cannot do.

But I understand.
It entered them.
Adventures of times past.
Mystery, never ending.
Romance, past and present.
History still alive.
A glimpse of what was.

Aviles Street

Standing beneath
the ancient archway,
I am jealous
of the old cracking
stones,
of what they have
seen, heard.
I am alone here,
but not lonely;
the past shares
my solitude
as I seek
secrets stored
in these stones.
Moving down this,
the oldest of streets,
on rough, uneven
bricks, I watch
shadows dance
over the moonlit
old hospital
and reflect
on the volumes
about those
times in the
library further down
guarded by that society.
I can smell ghosts
as I move forward
to the past, and
I am jealous.

Imagine

I have discovered
on some Old Town streets,
those fronting ancient
shops and houses,
where bricks and cobblestone meet,

against a misty dawn,
one can imagine sights
and sounds of times past
before manicured lawns.

Emerging from ornate houses,
well-brushed, mustached gentlemen
in stiff white collars
off to their shops.

Snorting, morning sounds
of an old horse, withers
trembling, warming to
the day's work.

The smell of smoke
off the bay front,
rising from an old barrel
warming boat workers
huddled amongst great pilings,
surrounded by shrieking gulls.

The haunting sound
of a foghorn,
announcing the start
of another day's ritual,
echoing through
the small streets and
alleys of Old Town.

Tolomato

Tread softly
over this small tract,
be mindful of what it is,
what it holds within
hallowed ground.
The story of this place,
this oldest city,
is here,
in the ashes of
Guale, Timucua,
Spanish, English, slaves,
Minorcan ... others.
Some notable,
some not.
Stand quietly.
Feel the centuries
Course through your
mortal soul.
Listen for a sound,
search within for
a sign.
 It is here,
with all these hundreds,
life extinguished into
the history that lives
in this place.

Oldest Drugstore

Through the street window
of that old store,
trapped by ancient
panes in wooden,
over-polished cabinets,
can be seen the
cure-alls dispensed by
Speissegger and Gomass.
Castor oil. Rose water.
Chills and fever tonic.
St. Augustine's famous remedy
to prevent all manner of maladies.
Potent medicines, Indian herbs,
And if all else failed,
concoctions known
only to the apothecary,
mixed carefully with
mortar and pestle.
Potions, lotions, and remedies!
Old, wooden floors creak
under the weight of ghosts
inspecting dark bottles boasting
labels of cure and guarantee
in the lingering, antiseptic smell
permeating air thick with
wisps of the past.

Old Jail

Cold steel and brick camouflaged
by that wealthy railroad magnate
with stucco, in Queen Ann style.

Matching the playhouse of
rich friends on holiday, some
forsaking afternoon tennis to
hear the gallows' door thump.

No view through those barred windows.
Floors and walls blank,
causing memory and fantasy to merge.

Thoughts of escape
from that plank bed
and threadbare cover,
but failure would conjure
more indignities from
slow-witted, ungrateful guards.

Tasteless food and rusty water
to pamper what spirits left,
taken with emancipated reason.
Savored slowly over the
objections of visiting mice and
amusement of the spinning spider.

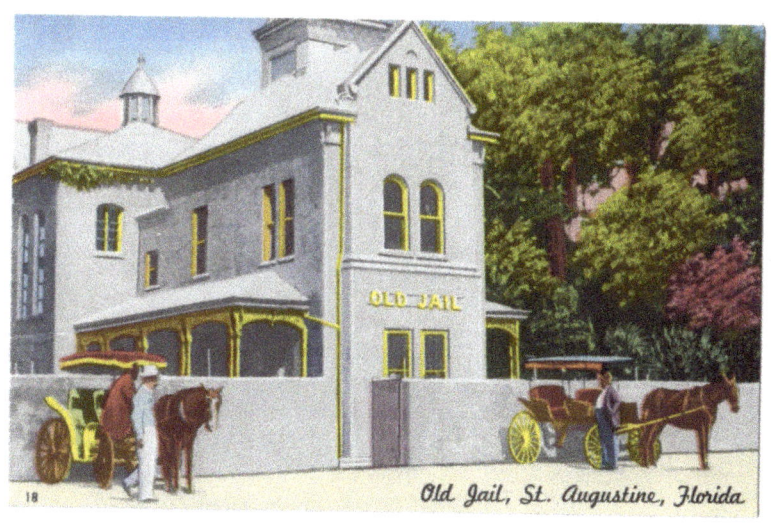

Old Town Streets

Giant, ancient trees
stand silently in
yards among
those old houses,
watching over ghosts
of gentlemen suitors
walking stiffly up
stone steps
to the sound of
music through
an open door
and the slow plodding
of a passing carriage.

Ghosts are walking.
Their movements cause
garden flowers
to rustle slightly
spreading a pleasant fragrance
through the air
surrounding mustached gentlemen
and refined ladies
strolling arm in arm
through the Old Town Streets.

CHARLOTTE STREET, ST. AUGUSTINE, FLA.

King Street and Plaza, St. Augustine, Fla.

Castillo De San Marcos

The Castillo would not fall.
Coquina carefully laid, each wall;
cut from rock of sand and shell,
by peons in the island quarry that was hell,
   and the Castillo would not fall.

Pried from the island floor with timbers tall,
across the inlet they would haul;
pulling, tugging with calloused hands,
footprints left deep in hot sand,
   and the Castillo would not fall.

Bastioned, parts snaking from the main wall,
making each tower appear small;
made so for lookouts to give the cry
if their flag the approaching ship did not fly,
   and the Castillo would not fall.

Some vibration, a thud, from cannon ball
hurled from ships to that wall,
once, relentless for thirty days,
'til that Brit sailed away on friendlier waves;
and the Castillo would not fall.

Over centuries, many tried; Brits, Gauls,
to penetrate that bastioned wall;
pounding storms, driving rain,
tourists' footsteps, all the same,
   the Castillo will not fall.

Lighthouse Porch

Early one morning while
seeking solitude on the
old lighthouse porch,
a pleasant sound
floated into my ear;
not yet dawn, only
distant sounds from
the inlet.
Quiet.
My reason for being here.

I searched among the trees,
still sparkling from dew
in the pale light, and finally,
as dawn gave way to day,
I glimpsed a small bird
just as it fluttered away,
and with it the song.
One lone branch, the stage,
like a conductor's wand
swayed to and fro;
happiness flown away.
And sorry was I
it chose to go.

Oldest House

I stoop to pass through
the modest doorway
and smell ghosts
of the artillery man
and feel the movement
of Mary's transient
guests.
Generations of Alvarez.
A glance at sparse
furnishings.
The tour guide's
voice is barely
audible.
For that is not what I want.
I want this room.
The sense of it,
rooted in a million
past footsteps.
I'm jealous
Of what I cannot
see; hear.
Fulfilled dreams not witnessed.
But I feel it,
in the rock hard wood,
the air, full of life,
holding the past.

Lasting

Carriages
can't be replaced.
Trains came.
Busses came.
Taxis came.
Still, the horses
plod along, pulling the
carriages,
at a snail's pace,
with aroma.
Not defiant
or humble.
Just here.
Everywhere.
Plodding along.
Not necessary.
But then, neither
Is the Fort or
that old Ponce place.
To pave over
nostalgic, old
brick or cobblestone
is ... unthinkable.
So, too, is banishing
the carriages that fit
the narrow twists
and turns of those
streets, with the
banter of all that
is the Old Town.

Plaza Beginning

We can thank
that Spanish King
four centuries ago
for declaring La Florida
towns outward from
center plazas would go.

The hub of activity;
all manner of goods
brought in for sale
to eager buyers summoned
forth by the sound
of the King's bell.

From narrow,
cobbled streets,
they would heed the call,
passing under overhanging
balconies through the scent
of lush gardens behind
stone patio walls.

Even now it beckons
to all who come,
traversing worn streets
to the center
of all things old;
the place to meet.

Renovation

What fascination we have
re-making the old houses
of the ancient city.
Workers treading cautiously
across thin planks supported
precariously by a woven
tangle of iron.
Blue gauze air, laces
of light bending through
ancient panes.
High, peaked ceilings with
the smells of times past,
walls soaked with
residue from countless
cookings; blending
of food, burning wood, charcoal,
oil.
It's work. But love too.
Strong calves and thighs
flicker from constant
stooping, climbing.
eyes sting from
sweat, slippery tools
hard to hold.

With the late sky
dimming through old
slatted vents, tired
workmen snake down
the scaffolds like grey
spiders, carefully. No net.
A dangerous business,
re-making the old.
Preserving history.
With love.
Making old new;
  But old...

Oldest Schoolhouse

Were they here, now, those
students of a time far away,
youth of the Old Town,
what would they say?
Sequestered within these old walls,
tempted by the smell of the sea,
learning the alphabet, A to Z,
what did they see?
What could they tell me?

Scratching of pencils
on slate boards again and again,
the swift rap on knuckles
for the smallest sin
from a strict headmaster,
where discipline was the rule
and for those daily hours
only one reigned; nobody's fool.

After the three "Rs",
how many stayed in this place?
How many chose to leave
with undue haste?
What stories of the Old Town
would they tell me, or you,
of those times, this place?
if only we knew.

OLDEST SCHOOL HOUSE, SHOWING OLDEST CLASS ROOM IN THE U.S., ST. AUGUSTINE, FLA.

Fountain of Youth

Keepers of that fountain
from which water flows freely
from the earth, clear and cool,
allude to its mystical power,
giver of eternal life.

For his king, Ponce, explorer
of small stature and large dreams,
claimed this land, this La Florida,
and sought the origin, and truth,
of the tale, then sailed away,

to return years later
to dislodge others and
continue the quest, but found
instead that crude, shell tipped
staff lodged deep into his body.

Three stately Spanish galleons
slicing through green waters
away from this land,
laden with its fruit, fresh meat,
and cool water, life ebbing slowly
from the conqueror.

Bridge of Lions

That old bridge
graced by lions,
struggling against
pounding wheels,
the elements,
and time.

The vague sea,
calmed somewhat
as the inlet
it has become creeps
further in,
nipping at the great
columns relentlessly,
year after year pushed
by tide and wind.

Unchanged, save for
the seasonal follies
of man, when the
great spans are adorned
with first lights, then flags,
now banners;
still the same.

Adored, even when
its rusty hinges
and grease filled
gears force open
its cavernous mouth
without shame
for that distant sail,
when it becomes the
bridge of pain.

Nombre de Dios

I gaze up,
awestruck,
at the imposing
symbol of Christianity.
'Name of God'.
First mission
of this land.
I watch as it
slices the sun,
causing rays of
silver light to dance
before my eyes.
I sense ghosts
of holy water
where gentle men
went into the
wilderness with
its spirit,
unafraid.
I sense miracles
and I am humbled.

St. Johns River

Ancient river, now calm,
at peace,
haven for all manner
of fish, fowl, beast.
Cypress lined shores
hedged with green,
movement among
massive roots, unseen.
You reach into swamps
flowing backward from the south
among dense trees
shielding the moccasin's
swift, white mouth;
where gator backs
and logs blend,
unfettered by northeast winds.
Masterpiece of sunsets
Reflecting over the
vastness before me,
into the wetness,
each different,
so many more
will I never see.
Your lapping water
tugs at my soul,
mixed with ancient chants,
stories told and re-told,
around campfires
of moss and stone
hidden below your surface
among charred bone.

My course is fragile,
a ripple that fades away
as I move on,
like so many before
who walked your banks
and then were gone.
But you are permanent,
flowing north, forever,
into that vast ocean
where your end is never.

Barracks

Before the Old
Town was so old,
in a time past,
when life was gentle,
the pace not so fast,
with the close
of each day,
near the south end
just off the bay,

on St. Francis Street,
the strollers would meet,

and in the last dance
of lingering shade
soldiers would march,
in full dress parade.

Townspeople and visitors
alike would stand
as cadence was called
to music from the barracks' band.

Reflections off brass
in the dimming light;
music, conversation, and laughter,
blending with the night.

Bartram Trail Incident

Just out of town
along the river,
on that trail, Bartram,
in 1840, a traveling troupe,
under the moon, silver,

headed to a performance
in the Old Town,
encountered a band of hostiles,
wild from drink,
yelping strange sounds.

Educated thespians,
city bred,
not comprehending their plight,
found themselves dead
on that cool, pleasant night.

But justice would
soon prevail,
from the end of ropes
at the oldest jail.

It seems there was no
need for any to confess,
because the hostiles, you see,
came to town , and in
the troupe's costumes
they were dressed.

Lovers' Wall

Tourists note with
some relief when
walking our ancient seawall
that it is ample
in width, giving little
chance one might fall.

For this, it is young,
star struck Captain
Dancy we can thank,
creating that spacious
path along the gurgling
foam of the ocean's bank.

He did so
not from necessity
or some engineer's test,
but, rather, from a
need he felt that
two should walk abreast.

The captain you see,
was in love,
struck hard by
the moon above,
and when strolling with
his lady along the tide,
he figured how neat it
would be to walk side by side.

Spanish Military Hospital

No blinking monitors,
I-V's, or nurse
call buttons here,
in this place where the
sight of crude instruments
could bring a tear.
Soldiers with some
malady, or perhaps
wound from a sword,
lay under the surgeon's
scrutiny on a
bed of board.
A place, no doubt,
they did not choose
to long tarry,
awaiting the herbs
and medicines of
the apothecary!

Menendez

A smuggler once, not
unfamiliar with the inside of a jail,
but all was forgiven by a king
bent on conquest and seeing no
match for this admiral under sail.

Weary from too many campaigns, the
fire within barely burned,
but from the shores of that place,
that La Florida, his son had not returned.
Amidst hope, perhaps meant to be,
he looked again to his beloved sea.

Opposing flags on galleons dipping
through the cold green water
atop sails strained by urgency
to be first arrived;
with pomp and circumstance
befitting the rituals of his land,
he stepped ashore, in fifteen sixty-five.

The smuggler-turned governor
and Captain General placed
a cross for his king,
and recalling his beloved Aviles
proclaimed this place after
its patron saint – Augustine.

FOUNDING OF ST. AUGUSTINE, FLORIDA BY SPANISH UNDER MENENDEZ IN 1565

Drake's Raid

In 1586, St. Augustine was
but a few dozen buildings, no
coquina yet, all made of wood.
A small timber fort housing
a mere handful of soldiers
on the bay peacefully stood.

Imagine the surprise of
the duty watch, hardly awake,
upon seeing with the light of day the
42 vessels of Sir Francis Drake.

The village alarm sounded,
artillery buried in the sand,
then to the woods those
few helpless souls ran.

With 2000 able bodies, the
Englishman had his way
with the sleepy little town,
plundering, looting, trampling
gardens, and burning every
crude structure to the ground.

Away the pirate turned
privateer sailed, homeward bound,
but from the ashes arose
a new, stronger Old Town.

Flagler

Second founder of Old Town,
builder of that railway
snaking down the
coast through towns and
marshland, along the
scenic, green wetness, bringing
his guests to a skyline
kin to Old Spain;
to the first of those
great hotels: Ponce de Leon.

A Coquina fortress
formed carefully
with that native stone
under terra cotta
boasting domes
and spiral steeples
that stood watch
over gala balls
and elaborate picnics
of northern escapees.

350 m. Alcazar Hotel and Cordova Annex, St. Augustine, Fla.

Chieftain

Proud chief, unbowed,
racked with the fever
of his land,

but unconquered.

Brought to that great
fort of stone
by trickery.

No treacherous general
could win the fight,
even with the great
Chieftain wilting in that
small damp room.

Dying in a different
land, far away,
on his terms,
painted.

Still no treaty.
Body among the worms,
headless. His presence
felt even now on moonlight
nights among the
stacked coquina.

Great Chieftain forever.

Whose griefs were many.
Whose trust was betrayed.
Whose waters still flow.
Whose land and people
still free.

Timucua

They were many.

Large, tawny bodies
bare, save for brief
patches of moss or
soft deerskin.
Adorned with simple
treasures of the land;
strings of polished pearls,
fish teeth bracelets,
brass ornaments that
tinkled with movement.
Tattoos signifying their place.
Sharing all things, taken
from the land with care,
with thanks given in
ceremony.
Sitting at day's end
around smoldering fires
under giant live oaks,
still in the coming darkness
with sleeping eyes, folded wings.
They were many.

The wind they worshipped
brought tall ships, blocking
their sun god's view.
Their words, strung together
like polished shells in patterns
passed on, father to son
became strange sounds
uttered by intruders.

Mystical names of the land
became as the others, recorded
like so much livestock.

Long, raven hair piled
high to taunt would-be
scalpers fell to the ground
with the great trees cut
to change villages to towns,
protected by a cross.

Then, there were none.

Ghosts

It is said there
are ghosts
in the Old Town.
Running amuck in
that old cemetery,
tipping ale in taverns,
pacing the floors of inns,
their spirits abound.
You may be a skeptic
or you may believe,
but for those wandering souls,
do not grieve;
enjoy their play
when you arrive,
these forms without faces,
keeping history alive
in all the old places.
And should you hear a noise
in that old house,
don't be alarmed,
it's probably just a mouse
scurrying away, causing
a creak in the wooden floor
and a moaning of old hinges
from the slowly closing door,
blocking your exit temporarily,
or perhaps, forevermore.

Carriage

Starting you is
not always easy;
harder on a cold day;
reluctant, leaving a
warm barn and sweet hay.

Once brushed, braced,
and hitched, your single
desire is to return here;
to that end, you
are always slightly in gear.

Your load, on wheels
of wood and steel, roll
freely on these hard streets,
though you abhor stopping
where two meet.
Your brakes are marginal,
in a perpetual state
of the near miss,
due in part to a
foggy state of bliss.
Your ears are immune
to the constant banter
of the driver guide
imparting old city history
to those along for the ride.

Others from behind press impatiently
from their steel steed, but
to no avail, for you only
have one speed; until
of course, the barn is in sight,
then those reins must be
pulled ever so tight.

Alligator Farm

I am Tarzan.
This path of boards
under my feet is
not there,
for I am swinging
on ropes of vines
over the large gator jaws,
open,
snapping, as huge
tails thrash wildly,
sending waves across
the jungle moat.

In this place
where birds flash
bright colors
through giant green
tropical leaves,
and snakes through
slit eyes follow
my every movement;
where Gomek roamed,
I am king;
for the moment,
in this zoological
park, this alligator
farm-this jungle.
It is all mine,
because you see,
I am only nine!

Early on St. George Street

I walked alone down
St. George Street early,
before
dawn and the opening
of shop doors
   and heard soft voices
   mixed with the clank
   of armor and clopping
   of hooves on cobblestone;
and passed on,
with the sound lodged
   in my head.

St. George Street

Every tourist who enters
the Old Town gates
will eventually stroll
St. George Street.

They are of every size and description.

Preserving the poetry of diversity.

Persistent,
moving ever forward,
an integral part of the
caterpillar that is this
mass of humanity.

Pigeons move deftly
among feet,
unscathed
by the sweat of
tightly packed captives.
Street smells.
Chocolate.
Displays announcing
every souvenir possible.

New mixed with
Old; blending.
Alive.

The Other End

I know a place
tucked away,
   secret.

Off the beaten path,
the opposite end of St. George,
   isolated.

Here, one can find quiet,
out of the hustle and bustle;
   solitude.

Shaded, calm,
benches for rest,
   or reflection.

An unkempt old well
for your wishes,
   or secrets.

Next to that old Inn,
the other end of St. George;
   secret...

REAR VIEW, SHOWING OLD SPANISH WISHING WELL, BLESSED BY THE MONKS.
OLDEST HOUSE IN THE U. S., ST. FRANCIS ST., ST. AUGUSTINE, FLA.

Finally

Enjoy the Old Town
in early morning
before you depart.
When her narrow streets
are unburdened by
the weight of steel beasts,
and the only sounds
are your footsteps,
echoing in small
caverns between old,
worn walls.
Without the distraction
of trolley bells and
tour guide narrative.
With only your thoughts,
your imagination.
Wander without
benefit of maps
and brochures.
Let the mystique
enter you and follow
your soul.

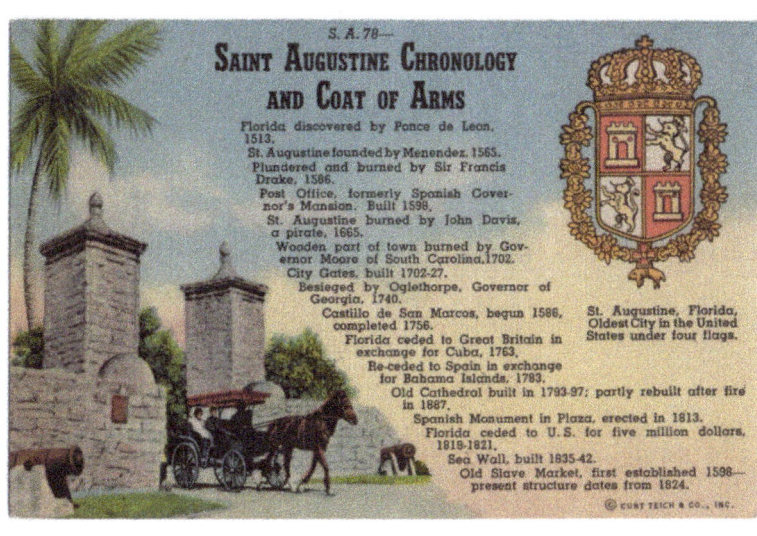

About the Author

Randy Cribbs, shown here with Murphy, is a native of Florida. A retired Army officer, he is a **2012 Eric Hoffer Book Award finalist, 2011 da Vinci Eye finalist, and Eric Hoffer Book Award finalist; a recipient of the 2010 FPA President's Best Book Awards Silver Medal for Young Adult fiction; a 2009 Moonbeam Young Adult Horror/Mystery Silver Medal; a 2009 FWA Royal Palm Literary Best Book Award; 2009 Eric Hoffer Book Award Finalist; two 2007 FPA President's Best Book Awards; and a 2006 FWA Royal Palm Literary Best Book Award.** He holds degrees from the University of Florida, Pacific Lutheran University, Jacksonville State University, and is a graduate of the FBI National Academy and the Armed Forces Staff College. He is the author of ten books, 6 of which are set in St. Augustine. More information may be viewed at www.randycribbsauthor.com; www.bn.com; and www.amazon.com.

www.ingramcontent.com/pod-product-compliance
Lightning Source LLC
Chambersburg PA
CBHW040325300426
44112CB00021B/2885